Mentor Guide for Leaders

By Amb. Prof. David K. Ewen, M.Ed.

I0480820

ISBN: 9798718988949

Imprint: Ewen Prime Company

Ambassador Professor David K. Ewen, M.Ed., TESOL, TEYL

About the Author,

David K. Ewen, M.Ed. is an ambassador professor to the nations in civilian business, education, and technology. He works closely with entrepreneurs, startups, business leaders, and government officials around the world. The ambassador has mentored youth and adults since 1985 and is the author of many books. Ambassador Ewen has worked in the private sector since 1985 and has been an entrepreneur since 1994 in Asia, the Middle East, Europe, Russia, Africa, Australia, and Latin America.

This book is written conversationally as it is a transcript of a produced radio broadcast yet to stream online. Read it as if you are part of a large audience enjoying a workshop seminar lecture.

The complicated world we live in is changing drastically each year due to politics, technology, and culture. The clashes that come from a growing population more connected by the ubiquitous internet and all its social media influences is growing too.

The way of mentoring is not the same as it was when I started in 1985. It's a different world today. A mentor must be more direct and forceful to get past the distracted influences suffered by the mentee. Especially today's youth that are overcome with digital communications that easily sway the way of the mind. The mentor must fight for the deliverance of the mind from influences. The influences fog up the difference between right and wrong. And wrong is slowly being perceived as right. A mentor can't be timid and must have the strength to punch holes through deception and manipulation that has overcome the mentee.

People are connected with IoT (Internet of Things) through 5G and free WiFi everywhere. The digital world grows with SaaS, Software as a Service that gives machine learning and edge on AI, Artificial Intelligence. It's hard to know what is true with AVR, Augmented Virtual Reality, that can trick our minds into thinking what is real is not. The danger of technology fooling us is here and the youth are vulnerable. Mentors must be aware when working with so many that are lost in today's digital age.

It is becoming more common that mentoring from seasoned professionals can help the struggling gain strength in the world they live in.

Mentoring is a kind of teaching that fits well into my experience. After earning my master's degree in education, I completed post-graduate business studies at a university before becoming an entrepreneur in 1994 followed by later certificate studies. The academic studies have built a strong foundation on what the world is perceived to be built on in terms of politics, economics, business, human resources, and technology. I have found that entrepreneurs can be effective mentors as they see the world in a broader way.

It was in December 2014, when I became an Ambassador Professor to the nations in the private sector at a time I really got to see the world in ways that I had never imagined. At that time, I had already been in business for 20 years and thought I had nearly experienced everything and of course I was wrong. So drastically wrong.

I am eager to share my experience as a mentor. The eagerness comes from responsibility produced by obligation. It's my time now. Mentors reach a point in their lives that they must give more than they receive.   Knowledge is supposed to be an outpouring of experience from wisdom.   Wisdom comes from mistakes.   I've made enough so I have enough wisdom to share.

Perhaps the most important lesson is that mentors need to be mentored. Another important lesson is that the mentorship process is not a process of negotiation.   From the mentee side, it may at first, but quickly the qualified mentor makes it clear that mentoring is not negotiating toward the fictitious needs of the mentee.

We all need mentors.   For me, I am mentored through our church with spiritual guidance that helps me with my daily life. The struggles and challenges of global entrepreneurship and ambassadorial stewardships goes beyond what I could handle alone without being mentored. Without being mentored, people can feel alone as I do with what I do internationally. That is why I give back because I see the importance of mentoring to people living in such challenging and desarate situations. Earth is not an easy planet to live on, so we need to help each other. Mentors have helped me and now it's my turn to help mentees.

The suggestions in this book may be a bit strong for some. It's OK. If I'm to share what the true role of a mentor of the changing world is, I'll tell it as it is from a perspective of experience since 1985.

I've become experienced to do my part to share experience in a mentoring environment. Perhaps it's my age and experience. Perhaps it's all the degrees and certifications. Mostly God. Perhaps all God. Yes, it is God. God gave all. I know that, but people I mentor do sometimes do not. That's OK. That's why I am a mentor.

The best way to talk about how a mentor becomes a mentor is to share a story. My story. It's the only one I know and it best illustrates the journey toward real mentorship skill and talent. The reason I feel natural in my mentoring process is because I have had a history. That history needs to be told so that others can feel natural in their mentoring process. Telling my story is not to toot my own horn in a prideful way. That's not the goal. Here in the book, I'll also share small tidbits of information. Well perhaps more than just small tidbits. Good stuff from true raw experience. That's what I will share and it's what you'll need to hear to understand the journey to mentorship. It's a long journey.

Winning awards for mentoring success is exciting, but after a few decades I thought it would be best to share my experiences that go as far back as the year 1985. That is a long time for mentoring and it's been a long journey with persistence and challenges. That is what creates wisdom. I need to share the decades of experience and also mentors must be thinking the same way too.

In the worlds of business, education, and technology, I have found the roots of success come from a solid foundation in mentoring. This comes in the form of management, parenting, spiritual guidance, and more.

While working at a data center as a quality assurance specialist in software development, I worked part-time as the assistant manager of a video rental store beginning in 1985. This retail experience gave me the opportunity to mentor youth who were reporting to me during the evening hours of the store's operation and during the weekend. It was here that I learned to encourage and motivate young people who were soon to graduate from high school and start on a broader experience in life at the university. I viewed myself as the important stepping stone to enter the outside world behind the comforts of living with parents. They had to learn teamwork and responsibility. What I had to learn was how to teach and encourage teamwork and responsibility and motivate their learning process.

My experience today is much different than the 1980s. Today I go through a mentoring process to motivate and encourage youth and adults in Asia, the Middle East, Russia, Europe, Latin America, and Africa. This changed experience involves a multicultural mentoring approach that is so different from what was done in the 1980s. That is not to say that the methodology applied in my days at the video store in 1985 do not apply today. The motivation and encouragement is a uniform language that is global. in all aspects of everyone's lives motivation and encouragement is necessary. The necessity of motivation and encouragement drives the need for mentoring which comes in so many different forms.

The best way to learn mentoring is to be a role model yourself. So many people in my early life were good role models. My mother and father together raised eight children and we're role models and mentors for all of us.

While in high school, I was on a sports team that taught me teamwork and I had a job at a supermarket that taught me responsibility. My advice to university seekers is to focus on developing teamwork and responsibility while they are still in high school. I do suggest the idea of being on a sports team or club and also to have a part-time job. The benefit is a coach on a sports team serves as a great mentor developing teamwork. The boss at a job develops responsibility. The result before entering the university is that the high school student receives mentoring in the form of teamwork and responsibility which is a crucial element that universities are looking for during the application process.

I don't know if it's because I have a master's degree in education earned in 1988 that causes me to put great emphasis on education, but it is true that education is a significant mentoring experience people need to go through in the early part of their life. Of course, great success comes from people without a completed college education, like the founder of Facebook, and I recognize and respect the "school of hard knocks". Yet, when a high school student tells me about the university they are thinking of, I go one giant step further. I also asked them where they think they might get their master's degree. I don't blink an eye; I ask the question. My discussion with the youth in terms of talking about university relates to continued education to the master's degree level. Today's children will be living in a more competitive world that will increasingly and constantly change in the area of culture, technology, and politics. Tomorrow's world that today's children will live in has challenges that we can't imagine today. Education is the safeguard to our children's future. It's something that can't be taken away from them. The education process teaches adaptation to change and that's the greatest skill of all.

I have always valued mentoring aspects of education; I find that the asset of knowledge is something that can't be taken away from you. For example, if you don't pay for your car or house, it will be taken away from you. If you are violent to your children, they will be taken away from you. But your education on the other hand cannot be taken away from you. That being said, it is important to get all the major core education out of the way before the huge responsibilities in life come into play.

What I'm talking about is that before you get married or before you buy a house or before you get that huge promotion and have such great responsibility, get your bachelor's degree and your master's degree and perhaps doctorate out of the way. This is the most valued mentoring that you can invest in that is carried with you throughout life. It teaches you the adaptability you must have in a world with changing economies, changing technologies, and changing culture. We live in a world of change.

What I've been discussing here is that mentoring should begin at an early age. The development of people in today's world is so complex with the various cultures and technologies that it is exceedingly difficult for people to know how to adapt to change. That is the biggest struggle I have when I meet with other people, both adults and youth. it all relates to change. As the world moves faster and faster every decade, I find that the world becomes more and more confused, and we see it in the news. This is why mentoring is so important nowadays.

As the world becomes more challenging even adults need the same kind of mentoring that youth need because it relates to change that is so hard and so complex. Many people have lost their identity and they misunderstand what a true relationship should be. For example, the Bible clearly explains the principle that marriage is between a man and a woman. In the world we live in today, that is not always the case because of the severe challenges people have with their own identity. This is one such example of how adults need to be mentored. They don't know who they are. It is also such an example where mentoring was lost during a person's time of youth.

I'm talking a lot about a very complex world that we live in due to changes in culture, economies, technology, and more. The world is in such a state of confusion, that we have forgotten what is right and what is wrong.

The only thing that hasn't been forgotten is what is right and what is wrong that is shown is the Bible, but nobody reads it. (shouldn't say nobody …. It's more of an expression to illustrate a valid point) That's why nobody knows about it. (Again,I say that as an expression) And if they do, they don't study it. That's because they don't go to church or visit with a spiritual leader to understand it.

(That's not an expression … that's actually true.)

We as a global community have lost sight of what is right and wrong so much that many of us think of the church as a bad thing. However, we know from history that that is not true. in years past, the church had greater value and authority that was equal to government. The pastoral responsibility of stewardship is a form of mentoring that has been misplaced and misused in recent decades. Hundreds of years ago, people sought after what God was looking for and followed the principles in the Bible to understand what was right and wrong.

My focus today is to talk about mentoring. It's not just what the church can do. The church does a lot. It's just that it's been forgotten. I believe that mentoring that gives a person the right direction can eventually lead them back to the church where they should have been in the first place. But my conversation today is not spiritual. Yet, think of this ... the importance of church being equal to government should not be forgotten. It starts in 1620.

When the pilgrims landed at Plymouth Rock in the year 1620, they set up a first set of laws for the community in that area. It was called the Mayflower Compact. The very first sentence of the Mayflower Compact in the year 1620 was, "In the name of God, Amen." This demonstrates that the first set of laws in the Northeast state of Massachusetts put God first before the government. hundreds of years from that time look at where we are now. We should be ashamed of ourselves.   Oh, I guess this is the part where everyone closes this book.   Again, such a shame.

If I think about the times the pilgrims struggled at Plymouth Rock in the first winter of 1620, I think about half the people who died during that time. Without any resources or food, it is fully understandable things that put in place with God leading the way. Everyone needs a mentor and therefore no one is following just man alone. Granted there is a hierarchy, that is why we have a mentoring infrastructure.   But there's always the top. Who is that? It is God. we manifest success in ways that go top down; that is to say from God to his people.

You might be asking why I'm writing a book about mentoring and including a discussion of how we as a global community have forgotten God. It is because God is the ultimate mentor and serves as a model of mentoring. If we don't listen to God, then we are not likely to listen to good mentoring. Because we're not listening to good mentoring, then we are paying attention more to confusion and division. you don't believe me? Read the news and you'll see what I mean. Some might say I don't notice anything. That is because they think the world we live in is what God had intended. They have become numb to the confusion, misinformation, and division that this world has to offer today.

I'm not punishing the Earth. What I'm saying is that we have an opportunity that we should not miss. Some might call it a needed revival. Others might call it a correction in our school system. Perhaps all definitions of a revival outside of a cult are correct. Either way it is something we are missing.

In my book "Boy Meets Girl", I talk about how families have been broken apart so that a child we'll miss out on the benefit of the combined mentoring of a mother and father. A mother provides the nurturing and caring characteristics that can evolve in a child. A father provides the lessons of responsibility, organization and discipline in their lives. The mentoring of a mother and father combined provides a solid foundation of confidence and encouragement creating self-empowerment. This is why children who are not from a broken home tend to have an easier path to success. That is not to say that a child from a broken home will not have a path to success. It just means that their journey may have greater challenges because they missed out on important mentoring that would come from the nurturing of a mother and a responsibility-driven father. They could have had the growing-up process easier if they had this type of mentoring when they were younger.

When mentoring is received at an early age it is more readily accepted at an older age and so the growth can continue to greater glory. It's best to condition the young mind to a state of receiving mentoring advice early. The effort toward correction is less and the distance toward greater success is shorter. Of course, there are exceptions and other root mentoring processes during childhood can manifest, but there is a point being made.

Let's talk about how an ugly word. Divorce. It isn't pretty. Now let's talk about simple basic facts. Divorce hurts children, but they somehow get through it. Single moms can't do it all, but they do what they can. Abuse is damaging, but recovery can happen. This puts a challenge on the youth of today. That's why sport teams, school clubs, church attendance, and a part time job can fulfill mentoring shortfalls from split-parents if there is such an environment of a broken home. The "working definition" of a broken home is where parents are split and have children. Divorced parents can testify the impact they have on their children (if they are honest with themselves).

Divorce, separation, and abuse caused by miss-mannered parents is an unfortunate growing trend here in the United States and around the world. That being said, it is necessary that a mentoring infrastructure be in place for our youth today and I have given some examples already. What I'm illustrating here is the importance of mentoring. The way that you can become a good Mentor is to first understand the importance of mentoring and the reason why it is important. By understanding the reason why mentoring is important then you know the purpose of mentoring which leads to a conclusion that is desired.

Now that we have an understanding of the need for mentoring, let's take a look at the people who can mentor. Let's start with the youth and their needs and who can mentor them. A sports coach at a high school can teach children the values and the benefits of working together as a team. This helps with the lessons and practice of communication and cooperation to reach a common goal. In another example, a classroom teacher can recognize behaviors of a child who is an introvert and hiding from the world and can somehow make corrections so that they're more expressive and able to communicate with the world. And next, a pastor at a local church can provide the nurturing and love that is missed from home and give guidance towards understanding responsibility and ethical behaviors. In all cases mentoring improves the character of how someone behaves and trustworthy communication. Did you see me use the word trustworthy? It relates to integrity which is an important part of a person's character.

A mentor is good at listening and searching for signs and cues that signify the root cause of an issue. This is an acquired skill that takes time to achieve. It is very much like the challenge of treasure hunting. It takes time to delicately dissect these search areas of a person's character and behavior to expose the root cause of pain or misunderstanding. Only true and raw life-experience along with fundamental academic understanding of human behavior makes mentoring an acquired skill.

At this time I'm going to talk about the six steps in mentoring. They are the following:

- Agree to Meet
- Meet Together
- Track Progress
- Generate Feedback
- Insight to Revelation
- Find Conclusion
- Next Mentor

The first step in mentoring is that the mentor and mentee must agree to meet. That means both parties have a vested interest in reaching a common goal. If one lacks interest, then they feel forced to be part of a mentoring partnership. mentoring is a partnership. One leads the other. The agreement identifies who the mentor is, who the mentee is, and what the goal is. Before any mentoring begins it is necessary that an agreement of a mentoring process be allowed to continue. It must be established that the mentee is fully devoted to the guidance of the mentor. Moreover, the mentor must be fully devoted to his duties in supporting the needs of the mentee during the mentorship process. Any shortcomings to this commitment result in a failure during the mentorship process starting on day number one.

After agreeing to meet with each other, the mentor and the mentee actually meet together in a place of convenience with comfortable surroundings. This could be a coffee shop. It could also be a conference room at a company. It could be at a restaurant. It could be in the garden at a park during a nice walk. Whatever the environment is, it must be chosen in a way that ensures listening and talking is done privately in a secure conversation. What I mean by secure conversation is the allowance of private information to be discussed without the risk of it being leaked out to anyone else outside of the mentorship process.

After the meeting you can get a benchmark of how other meetings will show progression towards success in reaching a goal. By the time you have completed the third meeting then you'll have a sense of how to track progress. If you never reach the third meeting, then you really never know why the mentorship process failed because the benchmark that was assumed in the second meeting never came to fruition to allow you to get to the third meeting which is intended to start tracking progress. Without progress tracked, there's no way to determine what the failure is. That is why step number one relates to agreeing to meet. It is necessary that there is a commitment for multiple meetings because eventually the progress will be tracked so that a trend towards success can be realized.

After the fourth meeting, concrete feedback can be given based on what was observed from the benchmarking following the second meeting and the tracking of progress following the third meeting. Concrete feedback cannot be given before the fourth meeting because a trend needs to be understood from the tracking of progress that is based on the benchmark established after the second meeting. This is why the original commitment to meetings is necessary for mentorship to be successful. Notice the logical progression.

Before I go on, let me review what we have already discussed so far and in summary. The first meeting is an introduction. The second meeting creates a benchmark of where the direction of future meetings will go. The third meeting is intended to track progress after three meetings have been completed. The fourth meeting is when feedback is given because sufficient understanding has been developed to allow for feedback to occur. The feedback that is given is valid because it comes from a solid foundation and avoids the mentorship process that began in the first place. There is a benchmark serving as a platform for discussion following the second meeting. After that there is progress that begins to be tracked after the third meeting.

After feedback has been generated and provided to the mentee success in the mentorship process is identified by the insight to revelation in understanding. This is when the light bulb turns on and I mean he or she finally gets it. This is the time when the mentor has finally gotten through to the mentee and the revelation of understanding has been met. Success ! And of course success does not happen in one day. It takes persistence through a logical progression of steps for a mentee to have an impact. Moreover the mentor and mentee are equally responsible for the actions toward success. But it doesn't end here.

The final step is to find a conclusion to the problem that needs to be fixed based on the inside to revelation in the understanding of what needed to be fixed in the first place. Whatever that conclusion is then steps can be taken to meet that conclusion.

The conclusion of a mentorship process isn't the end. It just means that the mint tea is ready for the next level of maturity in which case a higher level mentor is needed. It could be the same mentor who's able to address the issues at a higher level or it might be a new mentor altogether. Whatever the case a new mentorship process begins.

Not all issues that mentors and mentees entered are critical issues. Most of them are evolutionary growth processes. Examples can be seen from school teachers or sport coaches. These are long-term efforts by a mentor in coaching or teacher. The steps that are outlined are more of a formal mentorship process, but they're all very much similar. Whatever the case may be, there is a commitment by both mentor and mentee. The effort is not one-sided. The process is agreed upon. For example, the employee agrees to follow the instructions from the boss. The athlete agrees to follow the instructions from the coach. This student agrees to follow the instructions from the teacher. If we establish communication is not agreed upon, then no growth chords Revelation can exist and should exist if a progression of specific steps are allowed.. All mentorship processes start with an agreement.

A successful mentor has various characteristics that make them successful. The first one is the behavior of a consultant which is the most obvious one because it is the position where the mentor is an advisor providing suggestions. The second type of behavior is the one of a counselor where the mentor will listen and work to understand underlying issues. The third behavior is the one of a cheerleader for encouragement and support. So, in summary a mentor is a consultant, counselor and cheerleader.

Before each meeting with a mentee the mentor must have a lot of preparation in understanding what is going to be negotiated in terms of heading towards the goal that will enable growth and provide closure. Although I use the term negotiation, it is a step that is controlled by the mentor what is agreed upon with the mentee. the minty must buy into and accept what the mentor is doing. without that level of confidence, the mentee will not fully reach closure as intended. The mentor must meditate and organize a structure that has a clear path to the intended closure that the mentee needs. a person of faith will seek the holy spirit for this guidance.

Mentoring is not anything that is new. It is clearly shown in the Holy Bible indicating that mentoring has been around for thousands of years. It is not a simple process. I present to you five scriptures for you to meditate on over the next five days. This may allow you to prepare for mentorship.

As you read each scripture, take written notes on the page and mediate.

Proverbs 22:6 -- Train up a child in the way he should go, Even when he is old he will not depart from it.

1st Peter 5:1-5 -- So I exhort the elders among you, as a fellow elder and a witness of the sufferings of Christ, as well as a partaker in the glory that is going to be revealed: shepherd the flock of God that is among you, exercising oversight, not under compulsion, but willingly, as God would have you; not for shameful gain, but eagerly; not domineering over those in your charge, but being examples to the flock. And when the chief Shepherd appears, you will receive the unfading crown of glory. Likewise, you who are younger, be subject to the elders. Clothe yourselves, all of you, with humility toward one another, for "God opposes the proud but gives grace to the humble."

Titus 2:1-15 -- But as for you, teach what accords with sound doctrine. Older men are to be sober-minded, dignified, self-controlled, sound in faith, in love, and in steadfastness. Older women likewise are to be reverent in behavior, not slanderers or slaves to much wine. They are to teach what is good, and so train the young women to love their husbands and children, to be self-controlled, pure, working at home, kind, and submissive to their own husbands, that the word of God may not be reviled.

Ecclesiastes 4:9-10 -- Two are better than one, because they have a good reward for their toil. For if they fall, one will lift up his fellow. But woe to him who is alone when he falls and has not another to lift him up!

2nd Timothy 3:16-17 -- All Scripture is breathed out by God and profitable for teaching, for reproof, for correction, and for training in righteousness, that the man of God may be competent, equipped for every good work.

I pray for your success and prosperity. May God give you the strength and the energy to carry out your mentorship duties. May you have the strategy and wisdom guided to you by the Holy Spirit.   In Jesus name. Amen.

About the Author,

David K. Ewen, M.Ed. is an ambassador professor to the nations in civilian business, education, and technology. He works closely with entrepreneurs, startups, business leaders, and government officials around the world. The ambassador has mentored youth and adults since 1985 and is the author of many books. Ambassador Ewen has worked in the private sector since 1985 and has been an entrepreneur since 1994 in Asia, the Middle East, Europe, Russia, Africa, Australia, and Latin America.

Ambassador Professor David K. Ewen, M.Ed., TESOL, TEYL